# Content

Rise and Fall Shawl Page 14

Spring Brook Shawl Page 2

Wine Country Shawl Page 12

Atrium Lace Shawl Page 16

Spice Island Lace Drop Shawl Page 18

Ice Crystal Shawl Page 4

Lisbon Modular Shawl Page 6

Mill Falls Shawl Page 20

Triangular Motif Shawl Page 10

Sleeved Shawl Page 8

# Spring Brook Shawl

The perfect pairing of a pretty variegated yarn and open lace stitches makes this shawl a winner. An interesting edging technique creates a unique fringe along one side.

Designed by Ruthie Marks

## Finished Measurements

Wrap measures approximately 19" wide x 57" long (48.5cm x 145cm), including fringe

## Gauge

3 bridge sts = 3¾"/9.5cm; 3 rows of bridge/chains/bridge = 2½"/6.5cm

## Stitches Used

Chain (**ch**)
Double crochet (**dc**)
Single crochet (**sc**)
Slip stitch (**sl st**)
Treble crochet (**tr**)

## Special Terms

**Bridge st** Bridge stitch—ch 3, dc in 3rd ch from hook (first leg completed), ch 3, dc in 3rd ch from hook (2nd leg completed).

**Tr-bridge st** Treble bridge stitch—ch 4, tr in 4th ch from hook.

## What you'll need:

**YARN**
Caron Simply Soft Paints
(100% acrylic)
Shown in: #0004 Spring Brook (16 oz)

**CROCHET HOOK**
One size US H-8 (5mm), or size to obtain gauge

**ADDITIONAL MATERIALS**
Yarn needle

## Wrap

Ch 78.

**Row 1** Sc in 2nd ch from hook, *ch 2, skip next 2 ch, sc in next ch, [ch 4, skip next 4 ch, sc in next ch] 14 times, ch 2, skip next 2 ch, sc in last ch, ch 30 (for fringe), turn—77 sts; 14 ch-4 spaces; 2 ch-2 spaces.

**Row 2** Sc in first sc, ch 2, skip next ch-2 space, sc in next sc, [ch 4, sc in next sc] 14 times, ch 2, skip next 2 ch, sc in last sc, turn.

**Row 3** Ch 1, sc in first sc, ch 2, skip next 2 ch, sc in next sc, [ch 4, skip next 4 ch, sc in next sc] 14 times, ch 2, skip next 2 ch, sc in last sc, ch 30, turn.

**Row 4 (bridge row)** Sc in first sc, bridge st, skip next (ch-2 space, sc), sc in next ch-4 space, [bridge st, skip next sc, sc in next ch-4 space] 13 times, bridge st, skip next (sc, ch-2 space), sc in last sc, turn—15 bridge sts.

**Row 5** Ch 6 (counts as tr, ch 2), skip first sc, sc in center of next bridge st (pick up one loop from each of the 2 legs of the st), [ch 4, skip next sc, sc in center of next bridge st] 14 times, ch 2, tr in last sc, ch 30, turn.

**Row 6 (bridge row)** Sc in first tr, bridge st, skip next (ch-2 space, sc), sc in next ch-4 space, [bridge st, skip next sc, sc in next ch-4 space] 13 times, bridge st, skip next (sc, ch-2 space), sc in 4th ch of beg ch-6, turn.

**Row 7** Ch 6 (counts as tr, ch 2), skip first sc, sc in center of next bridge st, [ch 4, skip next sc, sc in center of next bridge st] 14 times, ch 2, tr in last sc, ch 30, turn.

**Row 8** Sc in first tr, ch 2, skip next ch-2 space, sc in next sc, [ch 4, skip next 4 ch, sc in next sc] 14 times, ch 2, skip next ch-2 space, sc in 4th ch of beg ch-6, turn.

**Row 9** Rep row 3.

**Row 10** Rep row 2.

**Row 11** Rep row 3.

**Rows 12-107** Rep rows 4–11, twelve times.

**Rows 108–114** Rep rows 4–10. Fasten off.

## Edging

**Short side 1** With right side facing, working across opposite side of foundation ch, join yarn in first ch of foundation ch, ch 30, sc in same st, tr-bridge st, skip next ch-2 space, sc in next ch-4 space, [tr bridge st, sc in next ch-4 space] 13 times, tr-bridge st, skip last ch-2 space, sc in last ch, 2 more sc in same ch.

**Long side** Working evenly across side, [tr-bridge st, sc in next appropriate st] 40 times evenly spaced across to next corner, 2 more sc in same corner st, turn;

**Short side 2** Tr-bridge st, skip next (ch-2 space, sc), sc in next ch-4 space, [tr-bridge st, skip next sc, sc in next ch-4 space] 13 times, tr-bridge st, skip (sc, ch-2 space), sc in last sc, ch 30, turn, sl st in last sc. Fasten off. Weave in ends. ▪

# Ice Crystal Shawl

Pieced-together floral motifs form a naturally curving wrap that hugs the shoulders gracefully.

Designed by Diane Moyer

## Finished Measurements

Shawl measures approximately 17" long (down center back) x 53" wide (measured along top edge) x 83" wide (measured along lower edge) (43cm x 134.5cm x 211cm)

## Gauge

One motif = approximately 8½"/21.5cm (point to point) x 7½"/19cm (side to side). Gauge is not critical for this project.

## Stitches Used

Chain (**ch**)
double crochet (**dc**)
single crochet (**sc**)
slip stitch (**sl st**)

## Special Stitches

**dc4tog** Double crochet 4 together—[Yarn over, insert hook in next stitch and draw up a loop, yarn over and draw through 2 loops on hook] 4 times, yarn over and draw through all 5 loops on hook.

**dc5tog** Double crochet 5 together—[Yarn over, insert hook in next stitch and draw up a loop, yarn over and draw through 2 loops on hook] 5 times, yarn over and draw through all 6 loops on hook.

**Notes**

**1.** Shawl is made from 19 motifs.

**2.** The motifs are worked in rounds and joined to neighboring motifs, using a join-as-you-go technique, while working the last round.

**3.** Work and join motifs in the order shown in the Assembly Diagram.

**Helpful Hints**

**1.** Motifs are worked and joined with the RS facing at all times. To keep track of the RS, place a marker on the RS after completing Rnd 1.

**2.** Marking the edges to be joined between neighboring motifs is helpful when joining a new motif to motifs already assembled.

## What you'll need:

**YARN**

Caron International's Simply Soft (100% acrylic)
Shown in: #9756 Lavender Blue (12 oz)

**CROCHET HOOK**

One size US I-9 (5.5mm), or size to obtain gauge

**ADDITIONAL MATERIALS**

Stitch markers
Yarn needle

## Motif 1

With A, ch 6; join with sl st in first ch to form a ring.

**Rnd 1 (RS)** Ch 2, 11 sc in ring; join with sl st in first ch of beginning ch-2; do not turn. Place marker on this side to indicate RS.

**Rnd 2** Ch 8, sk next sc, sc in next sc, [ch 7, sk next sc, sc in next sc] 4 times, sk last sc; join with ch 3, dc in 2nd ch of beginning ch-8 (joining ch-3 and dc count as last ch-sp)—6 ch-sps.

**Rnd 3** Ch 3 (counts as first dc here and throughout), 4 dc in first ch-sp (formed by joining ch-3 and dc), [ch 3, 5 dc in next ch-sp] 5 times, ch 3; join with sl st in top of beginning ch-3—Six 5-dc groups and 6 ch-3 sps.

**Rnd 4** Ch 3, dc in next 4 dc, ch 3, sc in next ch-3 sp, ch 3, [dc in next 5 dc, ch 3, sc in next ch-3 sp, ch 3] 5 times; join with sl st in top of beginning ch—Six 5-dc groups, 6 sc, and 12 ch-3 sps.

**Rnd 5** Ch 3, dc4tog over next 4 dc, [ch 5, sc in next ch-3 sp] twice, *ch 5, dc5tog over next 5 dc, [ch 5, sc in next ch-3 sp] twice; repeat from * around; join with ch 2, dc in top of first dc4tog (joining ch-2 and dc count as last ch-sp)—6 dctogs, and 18 ch-sps.

**Rnd 6** Ch 6 (counts as sc, ch 5), *sc in next ch-5 sp, ch 5; repeat from * around to last ch-sp, sc in last ch-sp; join with ch 2, dc in first ch of beginning ch-6 (joining ch-2 and dc count as last ch-sp)—18 ch-sps.

**Rnd 7** Ch 4 (counts as sc, ch 3), (5 dc, ch 3, 5 dc) in next ch-5 sp (corner made), ch 3, sc in next ch-5 sp, *ch 5, sc in next ch-5 sp, ch 3, (5 dc, ch 3, 5 dc) in next ch-5 sp (corner made), ch 3, sc in next ch-5 sp; repeat from * around, ch 5; join with sl st in first ch of beginning ch-4—6 corners, 12 sc, 6 ch-5 sps, and 12 ch-3 sps.

Fasten off, leaving a 6"/15cm tail.

## Motifs 2–19

Work same as Motif 1 through Round 6. Refer to Assembly Diagram, to determine placement of motif. Identify the edge(s) to which the current motif needs to be joined, then work Round 7 (joining round). You may find it helpful to place markers on the edges to be joined.

**Notes**

**1.** Hold motifs with RS facing you.

**2.** Depending on motif placement, one, two, or three sides will need to be joined to neighboring motifs. If joining across only one side, begin joining when there are two sides of the current motif to complete. If joining two sides, begin joining when there are three sides of the current motif to complete. If joining three sides, begin joining when there are four sides of the current motif to complete.

**3.** To join edges of neighboring motifs, ch-3 and ch-5 motif-joins (defined below) are worked instead of ch-3 and ch-5.

**ch-3-motif-join** Ch 1, sl st in corresponding ch-3 sp of neighboring motif, ch 1.

**ch-5-motif-join** Ch 2, sl st in corresponding

*(continued on page 22)*

# Lisbon Modular Shawl

Soft yarn, lacy motifs and a lovely autumnal palette turn this shawl into a fabulous fashion statement.

Designed by Linda Permann

## Finished Measurements

Wrap measures approximately 22" wide x 66" long (56cm x 168cm)

## Gauge

One motif measures approximately 7"/18cm in diameter from straight side to straight side; 8"/20.5cm in diameter from point to point.

## Stitches Used

Chain (**ch**)
Double crochet (**dc**)
Half double crochet (**hdc**)
Single crochet (**sc**)
Slip stitch (**sl st**)
Treble crochet (**tr**)

## Special Term

**shell** 5 dc in same st or space.

**Notes**

**1.** Weaving in ends as each motif is completed makes finishing much easier. A dab of fabric glue or fray check applied to cut ends will help prevent ends from working free.

**2.** Work motifs following the sequence of the assembly diagram, starting in the lower left corner of the wrap. Work the first row (8 motifs), then the 2nd (9 motifs) and 3rd (8 motifs) rows.

**3.** Motifs are joined in ch-1 spaces of the last round of each motif pattern, with specific instructions for 1-sided, 2-sided and 3-sided joins given below. In place of the ch-1 space on the working motif, insert your hook in the corresponding space of the motif to be joined and work a slip stitch, then continue crocheting on the working motif. Refer frequently to the assembly diagram to determine placement of each motif.

**4.** Refer to color and assembly diagrams before working Round 8 of each motif.

## What you'll need:

**YARN**
Naturally Caron.com Country
(75% microdenier acrylic/25% merino wool)
7 oz (A), 6 oz (B), 3 oz (C), 6 oz (D)
Shown in: #19 Vicuna (A), #20 Loden Forest (B), #18 Spice House (C), #22 Plum Pudding (D)

**CROCHET HOOK**
One size US 7 (4.5mm), or size to obtain gauge

**ADDITIONAL MATERIALS**
Yarn needle

## Motif Color Sequences

Work designated number of each motif using first color as first color and 2nd color as 2nd color.

**Motif A** (make 8): D, A.
**Motif B** (make 8): A, B.
**Motif C** (make 4): B, C.
**Motif D** (make 5): C, D.

## First Motif

With first color, make an adjustable ring.

**Rnd 1 (RS)** Ch 1, 12 sc in ring, join with sl st in first sc—12 sc.

**Rnd 2** Ch 1, sc in first sc, ch 3, (sc, ch 3) in each of next 9 sc, sc in last sc, ch 1, join with hdc in first sc of rnd (puts hook in correct place for working next round, counts as ch-3 loop)—12 ch-3 loops; 12 sc.

**Rnd 3** Ch 1, sc in first loop, *ch 5, sc in next ch-3 loop; rep from * around to last ch-3 loop, ch 2, join with dc in first sc of rnd (counts as ch-5 loop)—12 ch-5 loops; 12 sc.

**Rnd 4** Ch 1, sc in first loop, *ch 5, sc in next ch-5 loop; rep from * around to last ch-5 loop, ch 2, join with dc in first sc of rnd (counts as ch-5 loop)—12 ch-5 loops; 12 sc.

**Rnd 5** Ch 1, sc in first loop, shell in next sc, sc in next ch-5 loop, *ch 7, sc in next ch-5 loop, shell in next sc, sc in next ch-5 loop; rep from * 4 times, ch 3, join with tr in first sc of rnd (counts as ch-7 loop)—6 shells, 6 ch-7 loops.

**Rnd 6** Ch 1, (sc, ch 5, sc) in first loop, ch 5, skip next 2 dc of shell, (sc, ch 5, sc) in next dc, ch 5, *(sc, ch 5, sc) in next ch-7 loop, ch 5, skip next 2 dc, (sc, ch 5, sc) in next dc, ch 5; rep from * around, join with sl st in first sc of rnd—24 ch-5 loops. Fasten off first color.

**Rnd 7** With RS facing, join 2nd color in last ch-5 loop of rnd 6, ch 3 (counts as dc), 4 dc in same ch-5 loop, *(sc, ch 5, sc) in next ch 5 loop, shell in next ch-5 loop; rep from * around, to last ch-5 loop, (sc, ch 5, sc) in last loop, join with sl st in beg ch—60 dc, 12 ch-5 loops.

**Rnd 8** Ch 3 (counts as dc), dc in each of next 4 dc, *(sc, ch 1, sc) in next ch-5 loop, dc in each of next 5 dc; rep from * around to last ch-5 loop, (sc, ch 1, sc) in last ch-5 loop, join with sl st in beg ch—60 dc, 24 sc, 12 ch-1 loops.

**One-sided Join** (2nd through 9th motif) Work same as first motif through rnd 7.

*(continued on page 23)*

# Sleeved Shawl

## This unique garment marries the airiness of a wrap and the cozy warmth of a cardigan.

Designed by Lindsey Stephens

## Sizes

S/M (L/1X, 2X/3X)

## Finished Measurements

Width: 22½ (23¼, 24)"/57 (59, 61)cm
Length: 81½ (91¼, 101½)"/207 (232, 258)cm

## Gauge

In pattern, 15 sts (or 5 pattern repeats) = 4"/10cm and 6 rows = 4¼"/11cm.

**Note:** Each pattern repeat consists of a dc3tog and the following ch-2 sp, or 2 dc and the following ch-1 sp at beginning of rows.

## Stitches Used

Chain (**ch**)
Double crochet (**dc**)
Single crochet (**sc**)
Slip stitch (**sl st**)

## Special Stitch

**dc3tog** Double crochet 3 together—Yarn over, insert hook in next stitch and draw up a loop (first leg), yarn over and draw through 2 loops on hook (2 loops remain on hook); yarn over, insert hook in next stitch and draw up a loop (2nd leg), yarn over and draw through 2 loops on hook (3 loops remain on hook); yarn over, insert hook in next stitch and draw up a loop (3rd leg), yarn over and draw through 2 loops on hook (4 loops remain on hook); yarn over and draw through all 4 loops on hook.

## Notes

**1.** Body of shawl is worked sideways, from one front edge across to the other front edge. Openings are made for sleeves as body is made.

**2.** Sleeves are worked in rounds, directly into sleeve openings.

## What you'll need:

**YARN**

Caron International's Simply Soft (100% acrylic): 31 (38, 42) oz. Shown in: #9707 Dark Sage

**CROCHET HOOK**

One each size US H-8 (5mm) hook, or size to obtain gauge

**ADDITIONAL MATERIALS**

Yarn needle

## Shawl

**Left Front**

Ch 87 (90, 93).

**Row 1 (RS)** Dc in 4th ch from hook (beginning ch counts as first dc) and in each ch across, turn—85 (88, 91) dc.

**Row 2** Ch 3 (counts as dc here and throughout), dc in next dc, ch 1, *dc3tog over next 3 dc, ch 2; repeat from * across to last 5 dc, dc3tog, ch 1, dc in last 2 dc, turn—28 (29, 30) pattern repeats.

**Rows 3–42 (46, 50)** Ch 3, dc in next dc, ch 1, dc3tog working first leg in next ch-1 sp, 2nd leg in next dc3tog, and 3rd leg in next ch-2 sp, *ch 2, dc3tog working first leg in same ch-2 sp as 3rd leg of previous dc3tog, 2nd leg in next dc3tog, and 3rd leg in next ch-2 sp; repeat from * across to last dc3tog, ch 2, dc3tog working first leg in same ch-2 sp as 3rd leg of previous dc3tog, 2nd leg in next dc3tog, and 3rd leg in last ch-1 sp, ch 1, dc in last 2 dc, turn.

**Note:** Piece should measure about 29¾ (32½, 35½)"/75.5 (82.5, 90)cm from beginning. To adjust length, work more or fewer repeats of Row 3, and end with a WS row.

## First Sleeve Opening

**Row 1 (RS)** Ch 1, sc first 2 dc, sc in next ch-1 sp, *sc in next dc3tog, 2 sc in next ch-2 sp; repeat from * across to last dc3tog, sc in last dc3tog, sc in next ch-1 sp, sc in last 2 dc, turn—85 (88, 91) sc.

**Row 2** Ch 1, sc in first 29 sc, ch 25 (28, 31), sk next 25 (28, 31) sc, sc in each remaining sc across, turn—60 sc and one ch-sp.

**Row 3** Ch 1, sc in each sc and ch across, turn—85 (88, 91) sc.

**Back**

**Row 1 (WS)** Ch 3, dc in next sc, ch 1, *dc3tog over next 3 sc, ch 2; repeat from * across to last 5 sc, dc3tog, ch 1, dc in last 2 sc, turn—28 (29, 30) pattern repeats.

**Rows 2–29 (35, 41)** Repeat Row 3 of Left Front.

**Note:** Back section should measure about 20½ (24¾, 29)"/52 (63, 73.5)cm. To adjust length, work more or fewer repeats of Row 3, and end with a WS row.

## Second Sleeve Opening

Repeat Rows 1–3 of First Sleeve Opening.

**Right Front**

**Row 1 (WS)** Ch 3, dc in next sc, ch 1, *dc3tog over next 3 sc, ch 2; repeat from * across to last 5 sc, dc3tog, ch 1, dc in last 2 sc, turn—28 (29, 30) pattern repeats.

**Rows 2–41 (45, 49)** Repeat Row 3 of Left Front.

**Note:** Right Front should measure about 29 (31¾, 34¾)"/73.5 (80.5, 88.5)cm. To adjust length, work more or fewer repeats of Row 3.

**Last Row** Ch 3, dc in each ch and dc3tog across. Fasten off.

## Sleeves (make 2)

With RS facing, join yarn with sl st in sleeve opening at underarm.

*(continued on page 24)*

# Triangular Motif Shawl

A delicate floral motif connects daintily in this glamorous gypsy shawl edged with pretty picot scallops.

Designed by Lisa Gentry

## Finished Measurements
Shawl measures approximately 34" x 72"/86.5 x 183cm.

## Gauge
One flower measures about 2" x 2"/5cm x 5cm.
Gauge is not critical for this project.

## Stitches Used
Chain (**ch**)
Single crochet (**sc**)
Treble crochet (**tr**)

## Special Stitches
**Beg-Cl** Beginning cluster—Ch 5, [yarn over] twice, insert hook in 5th ch from hook and draw up a loop, [yarn over and draw through 2 loops on hook] twice (2 loops remain on hook); [yarn over] twice, insert hook in same ch and draw up a loop, [yarn over and draw through 2 loops on hook] twice (3 loops remain on hook).

**Open-Cl** Open cluster—[Yarn over] twice, insert hook in indicated st and draw up a loop, [yarn over and draw through 2 loops on hook] twice (2 loops remain on hook); *[yarn over] twice, insert hook in same st and draw up a loop, [yarn over and draw through 2 loops on hook] twice; repeat from * once more (4 loops remain on hook).

**End-Cl** End cluster—Ch 5, [yarn over] twice, insert hook in top of last cluster-group made (the loop formed by the final yarn over) and draw up a loop, [yarn over and draw through 2 loops on hook] twice (2 loops remain on hook); [yarn over] twice, insert hook in same st and draw up a loop, [yarn over and draw through 2 loops on hook] twice (3 loops remain on hook); yarn over and draw through all 3 loops on hook.

**Cl** Cluster—[Yarn over] twice, insert hook in indicated st and draw up a loop, [yarn over and draw through 2 loops on hook] twice (2 loops remain on hook); *[yarn over] twice, insert hook in same st and draw up a loop, [yarn over and draw through 2 loops on hook] twice; repeat from * once more (4 loops remain on hook); yarn over and draw through all 4 loops on hook.

## What you'll need:
**YARN**
Caron International's Simply Soft Collection (100% acrylic)
Shown in: #0014 Pagoda (18 oz)
**CROCHET HOOK**
One size US H-8 (5mm) hook, or size to obtain gauge
**ADDITIONAL MATERIALS**
Yarn needle

## Shawl
Ch 6.

**Row 1 (WS)** (Tr, ch 5, 2 tr) in 6th ch from hook, turn.

**Row 2 (RS)** Ch 6, tr in first tr, ch 4, 5 sc in next ch-5 sp, ch 4, 2 tr in top of turning ch, turn.

**Row 3** Ch 6, (tr, ch 5, tr) in first tr, Beg-Cl (3 loops remain on hook), Open-Cl in each of next 2 ch-4 sps (3 additional loops remain on hook after each Open-Cl is made), yarn over and draw through all 9 loops on hook (cluster-group made), End-Cl, (tr, ch 5, 2 tr) in top of turning ch, turn.

**Note:** When working into the top of a cluster-group, work into the loop formed by the final yarn over, and place the stitches between the End-Cl and the Beg-Cl.

**Row 4** Ch 6, tr in first tr, ch 4, 5 sc in next ch-5 sp, ch 4, (Cl, ch 4, Cl) in next cluster-group, ch 4, 5 sc in next ch-5 sp, ch 4, 2 tr in top of turning ch, turn—1 flower complete.

**Row 5** Ch 6, (tr, ch 5, tr) in first tr, *Beg-Cl (3 loops remain on hook), Open-Cl in each of next 2 ch-4 sps, yarn over and draw through all 9 loops on hook, End-Cl **, (tr, ch 5, tr) in next ch-4 sp; repeat from * across ending last repeat at **, (tr, ch 5, 2 tr) in top of turning ch, turn.

**Row 6** Ch 6, tr in first tr, ch 4, *5 sc in next ch-5 sp, ch 4, (Cl, ch 4, Cl) in top of next cluster-group, ch 4; repeat from * across to last ch-5 sp, 5 sc in last ch-5 sp, ch 4, 2 tr in top of turning ch, turn—2 flowers.

Repeat Rows 5 and 6 until there are 21 flowers across in the same row, end with a RS row (a Row 6). Do not turn at end of Row 6 and do not fasten off.

## Finishing

**Edging**

**Row 1 (RS)** Working in ends of rows across side edge towards lower point, ch 1, 4 sc in end of first row, ch 2, *3 sc in end of next row, ch 2; repeat from * across to lower point, (3 sc, ch 2, 3 sc) in lower point, ch 2; working across 2nd side edge, **3 sc in end of next row, ch 2; repeat from * across to end of last row, 4 sc in end of last row, turn.

**Row 2** Ch 1, sc in first sc, ch 6, *sc in next ch-2 sp, ch 6; repeat from * across, sc in last sc, turn.

**Row 3** Ch 1, sc in first sc, *([sc, ch 2] twice, sc, ch 6, [sc, ch 2] twice, sc) in next ch-6 sp; repeat from * across, sc in last sc. Fasten off. Using yarn needle weave in all ends. Block lightly, if desired. ▪

# Wine Country Shawl

## The prettiest little lace motifs crocheted in shades of red are cleverly tied together with tiny little bows.

Designed by Terry Day

### Finished Measurements

Shawl measures approximately 15¼" x 38" long (38.5cm x 96.5cm)

### Gauge

One heart = about 2½" wide x 2½" tall (6.5cm x 6.5cm)
Gauge is not critical for this project.

### Stitches Used

Chain (**ch**)
Double crochet (**dc**)
Single crochet (**sc**)
Slip stitch (**sl st**)

### Helpful

Weave in the tails of each heart as it is completed, to reduce the amount of weaving-in to be done during finishing.

### Heart

(make 96—32 each with A, B and C)
Ch 4; join with sl st in first ch to form a ring.

**Rnd 1 (RS)** Ch 3 (counts as first dc here and throughout), 2 dc in ring, [ch 1, 3 dc in ring] 3 times, ch 1; join with sl st in top of beginning ch—12 dc, and 4 ch-1 sp.

**Rnd 2** Sl st in next dc, ch 3, 5 dc in same dc, sc in next dc, sl st in next ch-1 sp, sc in next dc, 6 dc in next dc, sc in next ch-1 sp, sc in next 3 dc, 3 sc in next ch-1 sp (tip of heart made), sc in next 3 dc, sc in next ch-1 sp, sc in next dc; join with sl st in top of beginning ch—12 dc, and 14 sc. Fasten off.

## What you'll need:

**YARN**

Caron International's Simply Soft Collection (100% acrylic) 6 oz (A), 6 oz (B)
Shown in: #0009 Garnet (A), #0002 Harvest Rose (B)
Caron International's Simply Soft Paints (100% acrylic): 4 oz (C). Shown in: #0008 Sunset (C)

**CROCHET HOOK**

One size US H-8 (5mm), or size to obtain gauge

**ADDITIONAL MATERIALS**

Yarn needle

| | | | | | | |
|---|---|---|---|---|---|---|
| Row 1 | C | A | B | C | A | B |
| Row 2 | A | B | C | A | B | C |
| Row 3 | B | C | A | B | C | A |
| Row 4 | C | A | B | C | A | B |
| Row 5 | A | B | C | A | B | C |
| Row 6 | B | C | A | B | C | A |
| Row 7 | C | A | B | C | A | B |
| Row 8 | A | B | C | A | B | C |
| Row 9 | B | C | A | B | C | A |
| Row 10 | C | A | B | C | A | B |
| Row 11 | A | B | C | A | B | C |
| Row 12 | B | C | A | B | C | A |
| Row 13 | C | A | B | C | A | B |
| Row 14 | A | B | C | A | B | C |
| Row 15 | B | C | A | B | C | A |
| Row 16 | C | A | B | C | A | B |

### Finishing

Using yarn needle, weave in all ends. Shape hearts and press each heart lightly with warm steam iron, placing a cloth between the heart and the iron.

### Bows

Arrange hearts as shown in assembly diagram. Tie hearts that are side by side together with tiny yarn bows, as follows:
With B, thread yarn directly from skein through yarn needle. Insert needle through two, side by side, hearts where the sides touch. Leave several inches for ease of tying bows and then cut yarn. Tie ends into a bow and trim ends to desired length. Repeat this process until all side by side hearts are tied together.

### Assembly

Using yarn needle and matching yarn, sew lower tips of hearts to center top of corresponding heart in next row. Weave in ends after sewing each pair of hearts together. Notice that the hearts at the center of the shawl are sewn top to top (Rows 8 and 9). Once all hearts have been sewn together, press the entire piece again, on both sides, keeping a cloth between the piece and the iron, and ensuring that the bows lie flat and straight. ■

# Rise & Fall Shawl

## Shimmering chevrons give this wrap dramatic appeal.

Designed by Margret Willson

## Finished Measurements

Shawl measures approximately 22" wide x 72" long, 56cm x 183cm, not including fringe

## Gauge

In pattern, 1 ripple and 8 rows = 3½"/9cm
Gauge is not critical for this project.

## Stitches Used

Chain (**ch**)
Double crochet (**dc**)
Single crochet (**sc**)
Slip stitch (**sl st**)

## Special Stitches

**dc3tog** Double crochet 3 together—Yarn over, insert hook in first indicated stitch and draw up a loop (first leg), yarn over and draw through 2 loops on hook (2 loops remain on hook); yarn over, insert hook in next indicated stitch and draw up a loop (2nd leg), yarn over and draw through 2 loops on hook (3 loops remain on hook); yarn over, insert hook in next indicated stitch and draw up a loop (3rd leg), yarn over and draw through 2 loops on hook (4 loops remain on hook); yarn over and draw through all 4 loops on hook. **Note** Read carefully to determine into which stitch each leg of the dc3tog is worked. Some dc3tog are worked over 3 consecutive stitches, and other dc3tog are worked over 3 non-consecutive stitches, skipping the stitches between.

**dc2tog** Double crochet 2 together—Yarn over, insert hook in first indicated stitch and draw up a loop (first leg), yarn over and draw through 2 loops on hook (2 loops remain on hook); yarn over, insert hook in next indicated stitch and draw up a loop (2nd leg), yarn over and draw through 2 loops on hook (3 loops remain on hook); yarn over and draw through all 3 loops on hook.

**Note** Read carefully to determine into which stitch each leg of the dc2tog is worked.

**sc2tog** Single crochet 2 together—Insert hook in first indicated stitch, yarn over and draw up a loop (first leg) (2 loops on hook), insert hook in next indicated stitch, yarn over and draw up a loop (2nd leg), yarn over and draw through all 3 loops on hook.

**Note** Read carefully to determine into which stitch each leg of the sc2tog is worked. The sc2tog are worked over 2 non-consecutive stitches, skipping the stitch between.

## What you'll need:

**YARN**

Caron International's Simply Soft Party (99% acrylic/1% polyester): 21 oz (A)
Caron International's Simply Soft Collection (100% acrylic): 6 oz (B), 6 oz (C)
Shown in: #0003 Spring Sparkle (A), #0003 Pistachio (B), #0001 Vanilla (C)

**CROCHET HOOK**

One size US I-9(5.5mm), or size to obtain gauge

**ADDITIONAL MATERIALS**

Yarn needle

### Note

To change color, work last stitch of old color to last yarn over; yarn over with new color and draw through all loops on hook to complete stitch. Proceed with new color. Fasten off old color.

## Shawl

With A, ch 282.

**Foundation Row (WS)** Sc in 2nd ch from hook, sc in next 6 ch, 3 sc in next ch, *sc in next 13 ch, 3 sc in next ch; repeat from * across to last 7 ch, sc in last 7 ch, turn—321 sc.

**Row 1 (RS)** Ch 2, sk first 2 sc, dc in next 6 sc, *3 dc in next sc, dc in next 6 sc, dc3tog over next 3 sc, dc in next 6 sc; repeat from * across to last 9 sc, 3 dc in next sc, dc in next 6 sc, sk next sc, dc in last sc, turn—20 ripples.

**Row 2** Ch 1, sc in first dc, sk next dc, sc in next 6 dc, *3 sc in next dc, sc in next 6 dc; sc2tog work first leg in next sc, sk next sc and work 2nd leg in next sc; sc in next 6 dc; repeat from * across to last 9 sts, 3 sc in next dc, sc in next 6 dc, sk next dc, sc in top of turning ch; change to B in last sc, turn.

**Row 3** With B, ch 2, sk first 2 sc, [dc in next sc, ch 1, sk next sc] 3 times, *(dc, ch 1, dc) in next sc, [ch 1, sk next sc, dc in next sc] twice, ch 1, sk next sc; dc3tog work first leg in next sc, sk next sc, work 2nd leg in next sc2tog, sk next sc, work 3rd leg in next sc; ch 1, sk next sc, [dc in next sc, ch 1, sk next sc] twice; repeat from * across to last 9 sts, (dc, ch 1, dc) in next sc, [ch 1, sk next sc, dc in next sc] twice, ch 1, sk next sc; dc2tog work first leg in next sc, sk next sc, work 2nd leg in last sc; change to A in last sc, turn.

**Row 4** With A, ch 1, sc in first st, [sc in next ch-1 sp, sc in next dc] 3 times, *3 sc in next ch-1 sp, [sc in next dc, sc in next ch-1 sp] 3 times, sc in next dc3tog, [sc in next ch-1 sp, sc in next dc] 3 times; repeat from * across to last 4 ch-1 sps, 3 sc in next ch-1 sp, [sc in next dc, sc in next ch-1 sp] 3 times, sc in last dc; leave turning ch unworked, turn—321 sc.

**Rows 5–6** Repeat Rows 1 and 2; change to C in last st of Row 6.

**Row 7** With C, repeat Row 3; change to A in last sc.

**Row 8** Repeat Row 4.

**Rows 9–48** Repeat Rows 1–8 five times.

**Rows 49–54** Repeat Rows 1–6; do not change color at end of last row.

Fasten off.

## Finishing

Using yarn needle, weave in all ends.

**Tassels**

Make and attach a tassel to the end of each row, as follows:

With yarn same color as row, cut 4 strands, 10"/25.5cm long. Hold all 4 strands together and fold in half. Using crochet hook, *insert hook from WS to RS in end of row, draw fold through end of row forming a loop on WS of piece, thread ends of strands through loop and pull to tighten and secure. Repeat to attach one tassel to the end of each row, across both edges of shawl. Trim ends. ▪

# Atrium Lace Shawl

This delicate wrap, stitched in a subtle creamy shade, is equally appropriate for black-tie events and casual weekend get-togethers.

Designed by Donna Childs

## What you'll need:

**YARN**
Naturally Caron.com Spa
(75% microdenier acrylic/25% bamboo)
Shown in: #0007 Naturally (12 oz)

**CROCHET HOOK**
One each size US F-5 (3.75mm), or size to obtain gauge

**ADDITIONAL MATERIALS**
Yarn needle

## Finished Measurements

Wrap measures approximately 18" wide x 60" long (45.5cm x152.5cm)

## Gauge

*Gauge is not critical for this project.*

## Stitches Used

Chain (**ch**)
Double crochet (**dc**)
Single crochet (**sc**)
Slip stitch (**sl st**)

## Wrap

Ch 84.

**Row 1** Sc in 8th ch from hook and in next 2 ch, *ch 5, sk next 3 ch, sc in next 3 ch; repeat from * across to last 2 ch, ch 2, sk next ch, dc in last ch, turn—14 ch-sp.

**Row 2** Ch 1, sc in first dc, ch 3, sc in center sc of next 3-sc group, ch 3, sc in next ch-5 sp, *ch 3, sc in center sc of next 3-sc group, ch 3, sc in next ch-sp; repeat from * across, turn—26 ch-3 sp.

**Row 3** Ch 1, sc in first sc, sc in next ch-3 sp, ch 5, sc in next ch-3 sp, sc in next sc, *sc in next ch-3 sp, 5 dc in next sc (fan made), sc in next ch-3 sp, sc in next sc, sc in next ch-3 sp, ch 5, sc in next ch-3 sp, sc in next sc; repeat from * across, turn.

**Row 4** Ch 1, sc in first sc, ch 3, sc in next ch-5 sp, *ch 3, sc in center sc of next 3-sc group, ch 3, sc in center dc of next 5-dc shell, ch 3, sc in center sc of next 3-sc group, ch 3, sc in next ch-5 sp; repeat from * across to last 2 sc, ch 3, sc in last sc, turn.

**Row 5** Ch 5, sc in first ch-3 sp, sc in next sc, sc in next ch-3 sp, *ch 5, sc in next ch-3 sp, sc in next sc, sc in next ch-3 sp; repeat from * across to last sc, ch 2, dc in last sc, turn.

**Row 6** Repeat Row 2.

**Row 7** Ch 1, sc in first sc, sc in next ch-3 sp, 5 dc in next sc, sc in next ch-3 sp, sc in next sc, *sc in next ch-3 sp, ch 5, sc in next ch-3 sp, sc in next sc, sc in next ch-3 sp, 5 dc in next sc, sc in next ch-3 sp, sc in next sc; repeat from * across, turn.

**Row 8** Ch 1, sc in first sc, ch 3, sc in center dc of next 5-dc shell, *ch 3, sc in center sc of next 3-sc group, ch 3, sc in next ch-5 sp, ch 3, sc in center sc of next 3-sc group, ch 3, sc in center dc of next 5-dc shell; repeat from * across to last 2 sc, ch 3, sc in last sc, turn.

**Rows 9 and 10** Repeat Rows 5 and 6.

Repeat Rows 3–10 until piece measures 60"/152.5cm, end with Row 4.

**Last Row** Ch 4, sc in next ch-3 sp, sc in next sc, sc in next ch-3 sp, *ch 3, sc in next ch-3 sp, sc in next sc, sc in next ch-3 sp; repeat from * across to last sc, ch 2, hdc in last sc, do not turn.

## Edging

Sc evenly spaced across all edges of wrap, working 3 sc in each corner; join with sl st in first sc.

## Finishing

Using yarn needle, weave in all ends. Block to measurements, if desired.

# Spice Island Lace Drop Shawl

Dainty beads add a delicate shimmer to this sultry wrap, stitched in a drapey bamboo blend.

Designed by Andee Graves

## Finished Measurements

Shawl measures approximately 54" wide x 18" long (137cm x 45.5cm)

## Gauge

13 Fsc = 4"/10cm.
In pattern, 2½ pattern repeats = 5"/12.5cm and 4 rows = 2¾"/7cm
*Exact gauge is not critical for this project.*

## Stitches Used

Chain (**ch**)
Double crochet (**dc**)
Single crochet (**sc**)
Slip stitch (**sl st**)

## Special Stitches

**Beaded-ch** Beaded chain—Drop loop from larger hook, place bead on throat of steel hook, insert steel hook into dropped loop and slide bead onto loop, remove steel hook and replace larger hook in loop, yarn over and draw through loop.

**Fsc** Foundation single crochet (This technique creates a foundation chain and a row of single crochet stitches in one) –

**Step 1** Place a slip knot on hook, ch 2, insert hook in 2nd ch from hook and draw up a loop; yarn over and draw through one loop on hook (the "chain"); yarn over and draw through 2 loops on hook (the "single crochet").

**Step 2** Insert hook into the "chain" of the previous stitch and draw up a loop, yarn over and draw through one loop on hook (the "chain"), yarn over and draw through 2 loops on hook (the "single crochet"). Repeat for the length of foundation.

**V-st** V-Stitch—(Dc, ch 1, dc) in indicated stitch or space.

**Note:**
Shawl is worked from the neck down, with four increase points on each row.

## What you'll need:

**YARN**
Naturally Caron.com Spa
(75% microdenier acrylic/25% bamboo)
Shown in: #0015 Clay Pot (5 oz)

**CROCHET HOOKS**
One size US J-10 (6mm), or size to obtain gauge
One size US 6 (1mm) steel crochet hook for bead work on edging (or size to fit through hole of beads)

**ADDITIONAL MATERIALS**
8 stitch markers
33 beads (we used Darice Copper Metal Beads 825-2959)
Yarn needle

## Shawl

Fsc 29, turn.

**Row 1** Ch 3, (2 dc, ch 1, V-st) in first sc, [ch 1, V-st in next sc] twice, [ch 2, sk next 3 sc, V-st in next sc, ch 2, sk next 3 sc, dc in next sc] twice, [ch 2, sk next 3 sc, V-st in next sc] twice, [ch 1, V-st in next sc] twice, ch 1, 2 dc in same sc, turn—9 V-sts and 2 dc at each end.

Place markers in ch-1 sp of first, 3rd, 7th, and 9th V-sts. Move markers up as work progresses. Always move marker up to middle dc of dc-group or into ch-1 sp of V-st worked into marked stitch or space.

**Row 2** Ch 3, sk first dc, 2 dc in next dc, ch 1, sk next ch-1 sp, dc in next dc, **3 dc in next ch-1 sp, dc in next dc, ch 2, sk next ch-1 sp, 3 dc in next ch-1 sp, ch 2, sk next ch-1 sp, dc in next dc, 3 dc in next ch-1 sp, dc in next dc**, *ch 2, sk next ch-2 sp, 3 dc in next ch-1 sp, ch 2, sk next ch-2 sp, dc in next dc; repeat from * across to next marked ch-1 sp, repeat from ** to **, ch 1, sk last ch-1 sp, 2 dc in next dc; leave last dc unworked, turn.

**Row 3** Ch 3, sk first dc, 2 dc in next dc, ch 1, sk next ch-1 sp, dc in next dc, **5 dc in middle dc of next 3-dc group, sk next dc, dc in next dc, ch 1, 5 dc in middle dc of next 3-dc group, ch 1, sk next dc, dc in next dc, 5 dc in middle dc of next 3-dc group, sk next dc, dc in next dc**, *ch 1, 5 dc in middle dc of next 3-dc group, ch 1, sk next dc, dc in next dc; repeat from * across to next marked 3-dc group, repeat from ** to **, ch 1, sk last ch-1 sp, 2 dc in next dc, leave last dc unworked, turn.

**Row 4** Ch 3, sk first dc, 2 dc in next dc, ch 1, sk next ch-1 sp, dc in next dc, *7 dc in middle dc of next 5-dc group, sk next 2 dc, dc in next dc; repeat from * across to last ch-1 sp, ch 1, sk last ch-1 sp, 2 dc in next dc; leave last dc unworked, turn.

**Row 5** Ch 3, sk first dc, 2 dc in next dc, ch 1, sk next ch-1 sp, 2 dc in next dc, **ch 2, V-st in middle dc of next 7-dc group, ch 2, sk next 3 dc, V-st in next dc, ch 2, dc in middle dc of next 7-dc group, ch 2, sk next 3 dc, V-st in next dc, ch 2, V-st in middle dc of next 7-dc group, ch 2, sk next 3 dc**, V-st in next dc, *ch 2, dc in middle dc of next 7-dc group, ch 2, sk next 3 dc, V-st in next dc; repeat from * across to next marked 7-dc group, repeat from ** to **, 2 dc in next dc, ch 1, sk last ch-1 sp, 2 dc in next dc; leave last dc unworked, turn.

**Row 6** Ch 3, sk first dc, 2 dc in next dc, ch 1, sk next ch-1 sp, 2 dc in next dc, ch 2, sk next ch-2 sp, dc in next dc, **3 dc in next ch-1 sp, dc in next dc, [ch 2, sk next ch-2 sp, 3 dc in next ch-1 sp, ch 2, sk next ch-2 sp, dc in next dc] twice, 3 dc in next ch-1 sp, dc in next dc**, *ch 2, sk next ch-2 sp, 3 dc in next ch-1 sp, ch 2, sk next ch-2 sp, dc in next dc; repeat from * across to next marked ch-1 sp, repeat from ** to **, ch 2, sk next ch-2 sp, sk next dc, 2 dc in next dc, ch 1, sk last ch-1 sp, 2 dc in next dc; leave last dc unworked, turn.

**Row 7** Ch 3, sk first dc, 2 dc in next dc, ch 1, sk next ch-1 sp, 3 dc in next dc, ch 1, sk next ch-2 sp, dc in next dc, **5 dc in middle dc of

*(continued on page 25)*

# Mill Falls Shawl

The lovely openwork fabric and the generous length of this cape make it the perfect three-season coverup.

Designed by Kristin Omdahl

## What you'll need:

**YARN**

Naturally Caron.com Spa
(75% microdenier acrylic/25% bamboo)
3 oz (A), 6 oz (B), 6 oz (C)
Shown in: #0008 Misty Taupe (A),
#0005 Ocean Spray (B), #0002 Coral Lipstick (C)

**CROCHET HOOK**

One each size US H-8 (5mm), or size to obtain gauge

**ADDITIONAL MATERIALS**

Yarn needle

## Finished Measurements

Shawl measures approximately 72" wide (measured across lower edge) x 36" long (183cm x 91.5cm)

## Gauge

In lace pattern, 18 sts and 9 rows = 4"/10cm.
Gauge is not critical for this project.

## Stitches Used

Chain (**ch**), double crochet (**dc**), single crochet (**sc**)

## Special Terms

**shell** ([Dc, ch 1] 6 times, dc) in indicated stitch or space.
**sc2tog** Single crochet 2 together—Insert hook in next stitch, yarn over and draw up a loop, (2 loops on hook), insert hook in next stitch, yarn over and draw up a loop, yarn over and draw through all 3 loops on hook.

## Shawl

With A, ch 14.
**Row 1** Dc in 5th ch from hook (beginning ch counts as dc, ch 1), *ch 1, dc in next ch; repeat from * across, turn—11 dc, and 10 ch-1 sp.
**Row 2** Ch 1, sc in first dc, *2 sc in next ch-1 sp, 2 sc in next dc; repeat from * across, turn—41 sc. Fasten off.
**Row 3** Join B with sc in first sc, *sk next 3 sc, ([dc, ch 1] 6 times, dc) in next sc (shell made), sk next 3 sc, sc in next sc; repeat from * across, turn—5 shells.
**Row 4** Ch 3 (counts as dc here and throughout), sk next ch-1 sp, sc in next ch-1 sp, ch 1, sc in next ch-1 sp, ch 3, sc in next ch-1 sp, ch 1, sc in next ch-1 sp, *sk next 2 ch-1 sp, sc in next ch-1 sp, ch 1, sc in next ch-1 sp, ch 3, sc in next ch-1 sp, ch 1, sc in next ch-1 sp; repeat from * across to last ch-1 sp, sk last ch-1 sp, dc in last sc, turn—2 dc, 20 sc, 10 ch-1 sp, and 5 ch-3 sp.
**Row 5** Ch 1, sc in first dc, shell in next ch-3 sp, *sk next 2 sc, sc in sp before next sc, shell in next ch-3 sp; repeat from * across to turning ch, sc in top of turning ch, turn—5 shells.
**Row 6** Ch 3, sk next ch-1 sp, sc in next ch-1 sp, [ch 1, sc in next ch-1 sp] 3 times, *ch 1, sk next 2 ch-1 sp, sc in next ch-1 sp, [ch 1, sc in next ch-1 sp] 3 times; repeat from * across to last ch-1 sp, sk last ch-1 sp, dc in last sc, turn—20 sc, 19 ch-1 sp, and 2 dc. Fasten off.
**Row 7** Join A with sc in first dc, sc in each dc, sc, and ch-1 sp across, turn—41 sc.
**Row 8** Ch 4 (counts as first dc, ch 1), dc in next sc, *ch 1, dc in next sc; repeat from * across, turn—41 dc, and 40 ch-1 sp.
**Row 9** Ch 1, sc in first dc, *sc in next ch-1 sp, sc in next dc; repeat from * across, turn—81 sc. Fasten off.
**Row 10** With C, repeat Row 3—10 shells.
**Rows 11–14** Repeat Rows 4 and 5 twice.
**Row 15** Repeat Row 6. Fasten off.
**Rows 16–18** With A, repeat Rows 7–9—161 sc. Fasten off.
**Row 19** With B, repeat Row 3—20 shells.
**Rows 20–25** Repeat Rows 4 and 5 three times.
**Row 26** Repeat Row 6. Fasten off.
**Row 27–29** With A, repeat Rows 7–9—321 sc. Fasten off.
**Row 30** With C, repeat Row 3—40 shells.
**Rows 31–33** Repeat Rows 4–6.
**Row 34** With A, repeat Row 7.
**Row 35** Ch 4 (counts as dc, ch 1), sk next sc, dc in next sc, *ch 1, sk next sc, dc in next sc; repeat from * across.
**Row 36** Repeat Row 9—321 sc. Fasten off. Note: This is the final stitch count for this project. No more increases are worked.
**Row 37** With B, repeat Row 3.
**Rows 38 and 41** Repeat Rows 4 and 5 twice.
**Row 42** Repeat Row 6. Fasten off.
**Rows 43–45** With A, repeat Rows 34–36. Fasten off.
**Row 46** With C, repeat Row 3.
**Rows 47–52** Repeat Rows 4 and 5 three times.
**Row 53** Repeat Row 6. Fasten off.
**Rows 54–56** With A, repeat Rows 34–36. Fasten off.
**Row 57** With B, repeat Row 3.
**Rows 58–60** Repeat Rows 4–6. Fasten off.
**Row 61–63** With A, repeat Rows 34–36. Fasten off.
**Row 64** With C, repeat Row 3.
**Rows 65–68** Repeat Rows 4 and 5 twice.
**Row 69** Repeat Row 6. Fasten off.
**Rows 70–72** With A, repeat Rows 34–36. Fasten off.
**Row 73** With B, repeat Row 3.
**Rows 74–79** Repeat Rows 4 and 5 three times.
**Row 80** Ch 3, sc in next ch-1 sp, *[ch 3, sc in next ch-1 sp] 4 times, ch 3, sc2tog over next 2 ch-1 sp; repeat from * across to last 5 ch-1 sp, [ch 3, sc in next ch-1 sp] 5 times, ch 3, sc in last sc. Fasten off.

## Finishing

Using yarn needle, weave in all ends. ▪

 *(continued from page 4)*

Stitch this shawl in summery shades to match your prettiest party dresses.

ch-5 sp of neighboring motif, ch 2.

**Rnd 7 (joining rnd)** Ch 4 (counts as sc, ch 3), *(5 dc, ch 3, 5 dc) in next ch-5 sp, ch 3, sc in next ch-5 sp, ch 5, sc in next ch-5 sp, ch 3; repeat from * to corner at beginning of first side to be joined to neighboring motif, **(5 dc, ch-3-motif-join, 5 dc) in next ch-5 sp, ch-3-motif-join, sc in next ch-5 sp, ch-5-motif-join, sc in next ch-5 sp, ch-3-motif-join; repeat from ** around to corner at beginning of last side, (5 dc, ch-3-motif-join, 5 dc) in next ch-5 sp, ch 3, sc in next ch-5 sp, ch 5; join with sl st in first ch of beginning ch-4.

Fasten off, leaving a 6"/15cm tail.

## Finishing

Using yarn needle, weave in all ends. Block lightly, if desired. ▪

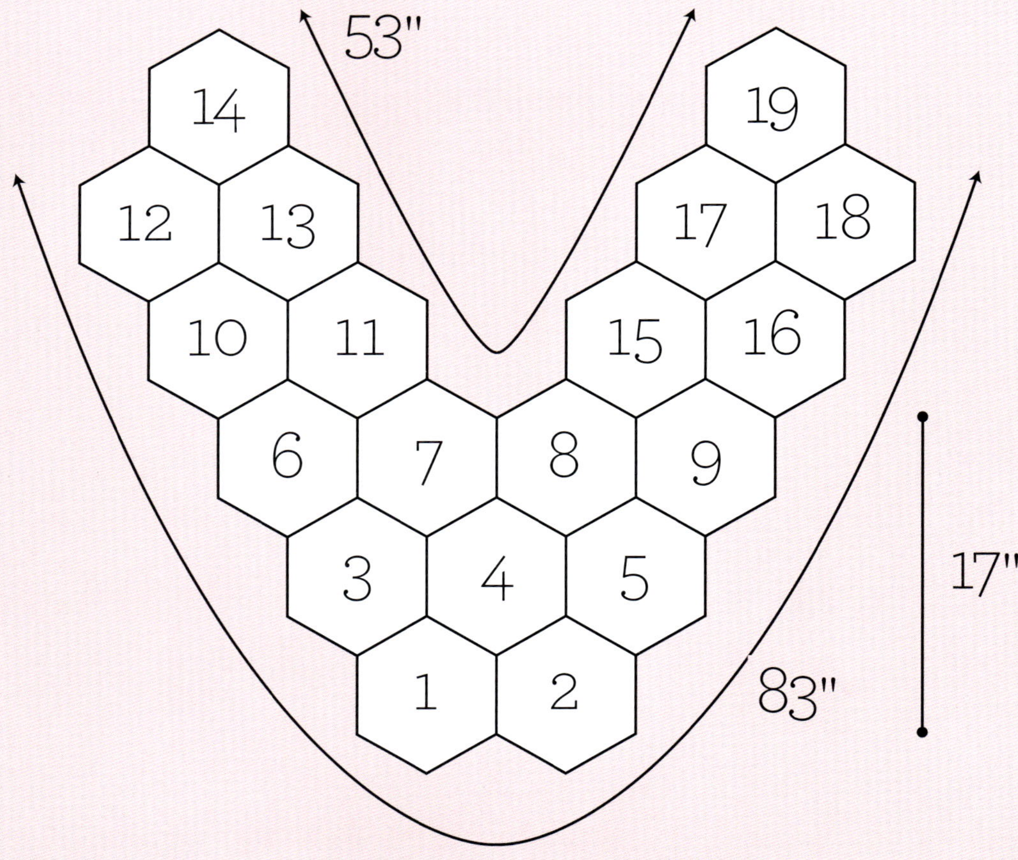

## Contrast edgings highlight the beautiful texture.

**Rnd 8** Ch 3 (counts as dc), dc in each of next 4 dc, *(sc, sl st in corresponding ch-1 space on motif to be joined, sc) in next ch-5 loop, dc in each of next 5 dc; rep from * 2 times to join, **(sc, ch 1, sc) in next ch-5 loop, dc in each of next 5 dc; rep from ** around to last ch-5 loop, (sc, ch 1, sc) in last ch-5 loop, join with sl st in beg ch—60 dc; 24 sc; 9 ch-1 loops; 3 sl sts.

**Two-sided Join** (17th through 18th motif)
Work same as first motif through rnd 7.
**Rnd 8** Ch 3 (counts as dc), dc in each of next 4 dc, *(sc, sl st in corresponding ch-1 space on motif to be joined, sc) in next ch-5 loop, dc in each of next 5 dc; rep from * 4 times more to join, **(sc, ch 1, sc) in next ch-5 loop, dc in each of next 5 dc; rep from ** around to last ch-5 loop, (sc, ch 1, sc) in last ch-5 loop, join with sl st in beg ch—60 dc; 24 sc; 7 ch-1 loops; 5 sl sts.

**Three-sided join** (10th through 16th; 19th through 25th motif)
Work same as first motif through rnd 7.
**Rnd 8** Ch 3 (counts as dc), dc in each of next 4 dc, *(sc, sl st in corresponding ch-1 space on motif to be joined, sc) in next ch-5 loop, dc in each of next 5 dc; rep from * 6 times more to join, **(sc, ch 1, sc) in next ch-5 loop, dc in each of next 5 dc; rep from ** around to last ch-5 loop, (sc, ch 1, sc) in last ch-5 loop, join with sl st in beg ch—60 dc; 24 sc; 5 ch-1 loops; 7 sl sts.

## Edging

**Rnd 1** With RS facing, join D in ch-1 space in top right-hand corner of Motif #25 (see Assembly Diagram), ch 3 (counts as dc), 2 dc in same ch-1 space ***, *[dc in each sc and dc across to next ch-1 space, (3 dc in next ch-1 space] 3 times, dc in each sc and dc across to 1 st before next joining sl st, work dc3tog over next (sc, joining sl st, sc) at junction between 2 motifs*, rep from * to * 6 times across top of Wrap, **[dc in each sc and dc across to next ch-1 space, (3 dc in next ch-1 space)] 5 times, dc in each sc and dc across to 1 st before next joining sl st, work dc3tog over (sc, joining sl st, sc) at junction between 2 motifs**; rep from ** to ** once, dc in each sc and dc across to next ch-1 space ***, (3 dc in next ch-1 space)]; rep from *** to *** once, join with sl st in beg ch—24 3-dc groups; 18 dc3tog.

**Rnd 2** With RS facing, join A in 2nd dc of rnd 1, ch 2 (counts as hdc), 2 hdc in same st, hdc in each st around, working 3 hdc in center dc of each 3-dc group, and working hdc3tog over (dc, dc3tog, dc–center 3 sts at each valley) around, join with sl st in beg ch—24 3-hdc groups; 18 hdc3tog.

**Rnd 3** With RS facing, join C in any st, sl st in each st around, join with sl st in first sl st. Fasten off. Weave in the ends. Block wrap to finished measurements. ■

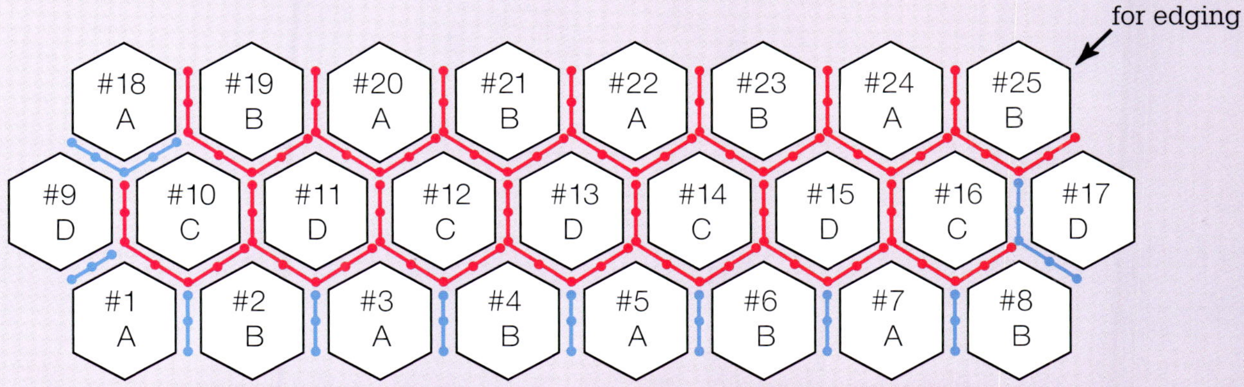


Assembly Diagram

 (continued from page 8)

**Rnd 1** Ch 1, work 52 (58, 64) sc evenly spaced around sleeve opening; join with sl st in first sc—52 (58, 64) sc.

**Rnd 2** Ch 4 (counts as dc, ch 1 here and throughout), [dc3tog over next 3 sc, ch 2] 16 (18, 20) times, dc3tog over next 3 sc, ch 1; join with sl st in 3rd ch of beginning ch—17 (19, 21) pattern repeats.

**Rnds 3–19 (20, 20)** Ch 4, dc3tog working first leg in first ch-1 sp, 2nd leg in next dc3tog, and 3rd leg in next ch-2 sp, *ch 2, dc3tog working first leg in same ch-2 sp as 3rd leg of previous dc3tog, 2nd leg in next dc3tog, and 3rd leg in next ch-2 sp; repeat from * around to last dc3tog, dc3tog working first leg in same ch-2 sp as 3rd leg of previous dc3tog, 2nd leg in next dc3tog, and 3rd leg in last ch-1 sp, ch 1; join with sl st in 3rd ch of beginning ch.

**Note:** Sleeve should measure about 12¾ (13½, 13½)"/32.5 (34.5, 34.5)cm from beginning. To adjust length, work more or fewer repeats of Round 3.

**Last Round:** Ch 3, dc in each ch and dc3tog around; join with sl st in top of beginning ch. Fasten off. Repeat for 2nd sleeve.

## Finishing

Using yarn needle weave in all ends. ▪

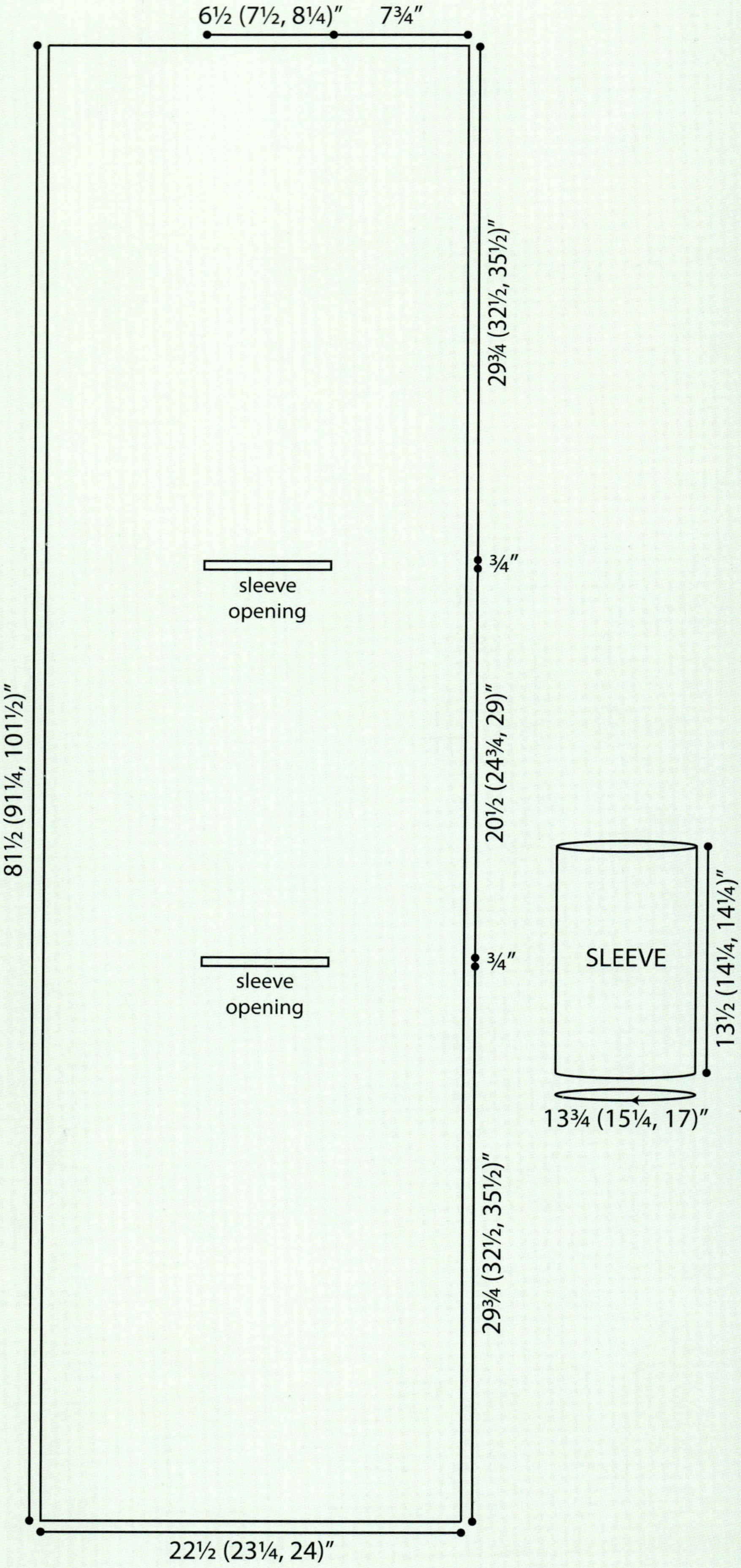